Swing trading Using the 4-Hour Chart

Part 2: Trade the Fake!

Heikin Ashi Trader

Table of Contents

A feint at its finest! 3

How to Identify Fakeouts? 9

How do I trade Fakeouts? 16

Fakes with technical chart patterns 22
    A. flags 22
    B. Triangles 24
    C. Trend Channels 26

Trading cross rates 29

More complex patterns 31

Glossary 33

Other Books by Heikin Ashi Trader 35

About the Author 37

Imprint 38

A feint at its finest!

Financial markets have become more efficient in the computer age. They are so efficient that they can afford all kinds of razzle-dazzle (feints) that put private traders permanently to the test. Technical analysis is no longer working, some argue. Algorithms and black boxes have so shaken up the game that reasonable setups can no longer be found, let alone that one could trade them.

These complaints are not new, and the question of whether the markets were easier to trade before the computer age, can be answered by only those who were there then and still trade today. These are not very many. The question should therefore be: can I look at the markets so that I can use the feints, the Stop Fishing, the games, and the algorithms of the Big Money to my advantage?

The answer is a resounding yes! With practice, you can find these tricks on a chart and identify the underlying intentions. You can even develop an extremely profitable trading strategy that is based exclusively on the detection of the so-called "fakeouts". Such a strategy would correspond to the realities of today's markets, instead of trying "to beat the market" with outdated methods.

Similarly, to swarm intelligence, all players in the financial markets have learned new lessons. However, although the complexity has unquestionably increased, yet the same patterns can be observed repeatedly. Although these are based on the usual rules of technical analysis, they lead them partly to absurdity, not to say, they play a little game with her and her expectations.

The feint has become the rule, which many traders who have eagerly incorporated technical analysis drives astray. With a slight exaggeration, one could say for today's markets: First the feint comes and then the actual movement. Those who recognize this as a small fish can go swimming with the sharks. Then, trading becomes again a real pleasure, what it should be in my opinion, no matter what some may say about the necessary boredom as good trading.

Who makes the observation of deception or fakeout be the first principle of his trading philosophy, observes at the same time the intentions of the major players. These ones ultimately lead the baton in the orchestra. To follow them has never been wrong.

One could say, "At their fakes, ye shall know them!" It is the big players that are able to break supports or resistances that have been built up over several days and to fish all waiting stop orders there and then to merrily drive the market back. Less capitalized individuals cannot do this. A picture is worth as much as a thousand words:

Figure 1: Crude Oil Future, 4-hour chart

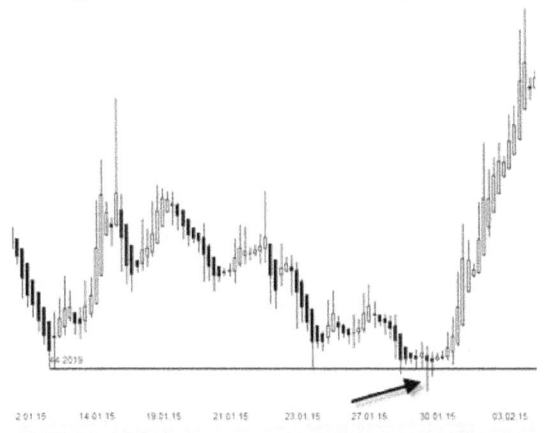

This example in the crude oil futures illustrates the above statement quite well. We see that the Crude Oil future found a support at US $ 44.20 on the 13th Of January 2015 (horizontal line in the chart). This support lasted about 2 weeks, and has been tested several times (8 times).

On January 29th, the market broke through this support (arrow) and the oil futures sank temporarily to US $ 43.57. This downward breakout would have triggered a short signal to the classical technical analysis, and I am convinced that many traders have actually traded this signal.

Maybe they got a beep from their platforms that "the market" had fallen below US $ 44.20. On the other hand, they had placed a sell-stop order below US$ 44.20. Such a decision is, according to the classical doctrine not illogical. After all, the futures had tested this important support in the weeks before a total of eight times.

In other words, all market players observed this support level and probably had - as I did - marked it with a horizontal line on their charts. The classic question was therefore: will the support hold, or will the oil price continue to fall?

However, it is exactly this classic question that is driving the untrained technical analysts astray. The smart money obviously, is well aware that the small players ask themselves this question. As the eruption on 29th January happened, the decision seemed like Short! Now, we see on the chart that this decision was wrong. The Future lingered a few hours under the US $ 44.20 level and soon returned. The closing price of the breakout candle was above the US $ 44.20 level. The alleged short signal was thus a deception because the closing price on a 4-hour basis should at least have been below the support.

The "bears" (the seller or short sellers) temporarily succeeded to squeeze the price under the support, but, the "bulls" (the buyers) had slammed immediately and had seized the opportunity to once again get into the market at low prices.

There were obviously more buyers than sellers, the price soared upwards again. This is visualized by the long shadow of the candles on the Heikin Ashi chart. Adepts of the candlestick representation will identify this pattern as a "hammer", which is generally interpreted as a bullish pattern.

Mostly though, you are more likely to find the term "Pin Bar". This is an abbreviation of "Pinocchio's Bar". In other words, the long narrow shadow of the candle symbolizes Pinocchio's nose, which means that here, a lie is told.

The downside breakout thus stood as a failure occurrence or deception. I will continue to speak in the course of this book for simplicity of "fakeout", the term used for this phenomenon by many traders.

Only large, heavily capitalized traders are able to break through such strong support, generally. One thing is clear: since all market players observe the support level for weeks, many bargain hunters are willing to buy the market as soon as the price comes closer to the support level.

Moreover, nowadays it is almost a rule that the big players like to play a little game with the kids by all pretending that from now (after the breakout downwards), a new phase has occurred, namely that the market will continue to fall. The bargain hunters who naturally hedged their long positions with a stop-loss order slightly below the support will be stopped out by the sudden fall of the price.

In addition, the stop-sell orders of the short sellers (these are the orders of those who bet on falling prices) are executed and drive the market further down.

That is the moment the big players have been waiting for! Because the sum of the story is that in many cases the so-called "sellers" and the so-called "buyers" are often the same actors. Before they have pushed the market down, they have long since placed large buy orders below the same stop-loss levels. Those buy orders intercept the market and it begins to rise again.

The short sellers suddenly realize that they have backed the wrong horse and they are urged to cover their short positions by buying back their contracts. This pushes the market further up and soon the market is back to where it was for weeks, namely above US $ 44.20.

After this shock, of course, nobody dears to go short again. The result can be seen clearly on the right side of the chart. A few hours after the failed breakout the market begins to rise in such a way as if there was no tomorrow. The oil price rose 10 dollars within a few days. The beauty of the Heikin Ashi candles is that the trader can identify this trend correctly.

The big players have had their fun and were able to realize huge profits after they had entered the market at almost 0-risk below the support. The feint was perfect. The small traders (bargain hunters and the short traders) were catapulted off the market with a loss through the fakeout and now dare not take a position again. The smart money has once again managed to round out the nose of everybody.

This phenomenon, you will encounter repeatedly in today's markets. One could speak of a basic pattern, and those who understand this can develop a very profitable strategy based solely on the observation of such deceptions or fakes. Besides my scalping activity of this pattern has become my daily bread.

How to Identify Fakeouts?

Feints or fakeouts can occur anywhere at all possible locations in the market, and they are not always readily apparent. I want to list some advice on where best to recognize and find fakeouts. You will find this is usually less in trending markets, especially when they occur at high volume.

This kind of market is very difficult to manipulate as market participants agree, in which direction they want to buy or sell the market. In addition, Trend markets attract the attention of tens of thousands of traders who want to benefit from the strong trend of course.

If you study the charts of markets that are in a clear trend, you will see mostly regular price development. This is reflected clearly in the candlestick representation and even better in the Heikin Ashi chart form.

If a market rises sharply, you will often see only white candles in the Heikin Ashi chart. According to the Heikin Ashi chart, it only records black candles when the market is in a clear downward trend. Such markets have a loyal following, as a rule, they are easier to trade and difficult to manipulate.

When the trend is over or has achieved its goal, the market usually gets in calmer waters and the volatility decreases. Usually it passes then, rather sideways or moves in a **"range"** as traders call it.

A range is nothing else than a zone within which the market for some time moves without any clear destination. The reason for the emergence of a range can be varied. After a strong trend, it is only natural that the market comes a bit "to rest". The news and the fresh fundamentals are now priced into the courses, and the market participants appear to more or less agree on the price at the current price level.

Another reason might simply be the absence of relevant news. In particular, in the currency markets, which are indeed highly news driven markets, the absence of major economic data, such as labor market reports or interest rate decisions often means that the currency pair goes sideways without large fluctuations.

Of course, this happens also when the market players expect the publication of important data. Many traders might not have a position before the publication. It then looks as if the market is floating with no clear direction. This is a market more for day traders and scalpers.

Every so often the price is jumping like Ping-Pong balls without leaving the range appreciably. Many traders who rely on trends, have no interest in this ranges and look for better opportunities in other markets where there may be better chances.

It is therefore important whether a trader is clear about what is right now at stake in this or that market. Is the market slowing down after a strong trend and now gathering force for further movement? Do the participants expect important news that will give them insight into the future direction of the market? Alternatively, is there nothing going on in this market?

As few traders are interested in a trend-less market, the volume is naturally lower. However, this is exactly the type of market in which the fakeouts preferably occur. If only a few players are involved, it is naturally easier for a midsize player to move the price for a short time in the one or another direction.

Especially when the price is at the bottom of the range (support) or on the upper side (resistance), it is tempting to feint a false breakout for a well-capitalized trader. He knows that there are always plenty of traders who are ready to respond to the maneuver. They therefore support consciously or unconsciously the almighty poker player in his intentions, for example by trading the fake breakout or sell again as soon as the breakout turns out to be a fake.

The poor old chaps are in this case those traders who trade the breakout itself. As soon as they are in the market, our omniscient trader rotates his position, and their position is in loss. Eventually they realize that they have backed the wrong horse, and must close their trades with loss, which naturally exert additional pressure on the market. That is why sometimes you see on charts after false breakout, quite spectacular sales.

It is more preferable therefore to wait for the breakout, and if it turns out to be a false breakout to act in the opposite direction. In a slight exaggeration, one could say: Amateurs trade the breakout, professionals trade the fake. However, of course care is always required. Not every breakout is a fake, and some are actually just the start of a new trend move. In this case, the trader should close his position quickly.

Since fakes preferably appear at price levels, which we call in the technical analysis, support and resistance, we expect therefore regular predictable price movements. A support means nothing more than that the buying pressure at a certain price level is just slightly higher than the selling pressure. Therefore, it does not mean that there are no sellers there. This should not be forgotten, even if the chart suggests that "the market" rotates here, it is far from that all sellers have suddenly dissapeared.

Nevertheless, I think that the concept of support and resistance continues to offer excellent trading opportunities, solely for reasons of risk-reward ratio. Many successful traders do just that: they buy support and sell resistance.

For whom this seems to be too easy, or who is of the opinion that there are just too many fakes in today's markets, should deal with the idea of fake trading. You could refer to a fake trader as a trader who monitors the events at support and the resistance exactly. If he identifies a false breakout, he immediately gets a trading opportunity, no matter how far or how close the target price might be ultimately.

It speaks for itself that many scalpers take advantage of this circumstance and are skilled fake traders. Nevertheless, if their price targets are naturally shorter than those of the swing trader are, they have the same intention and help to move the market back in the direction of the major trend.

I like to call the fake trader the shrewd trader who does exactly the opposite of a normal breakout trader. This trader simply puts a stop-buy above resistance and a stop-sell under the support in the hope that the breakout might succeed. This approach may sometimes work. More likely, however, this type of trader will be the victim of a fakeout.

A fake trader waits and watches how the events on the resistance and the support evolve exactly. If an outbreak happens, he observes this first. Is the breakout real, then he will let it run. He takes no position and certainly does not jump on top of the train. This approach he leaves to the beginners in the knowledge that this is most likely doomed.

If the breakout is identified as a fakeout, only then arises for this type trader, a real opportunity. You can therefore compare a fake trader to a sniper who can wait sometimes for hours for the best chance to take a successful shot. A fake trader is therefore naturally, a patient trader.

This does not mean that breakout trading no longer works. Breakout trading works very well and is a legitimate trading strategy. The breakout trader should however be a master to recognize false breakouts and try to avoid trading them.

Especially if the expected news is published, the breakout from the range often succeed and can transform a market in an almost never-ending trend for days. This, too, the trader who relies on false breakouts, should know. In both cases, the trader should definitely work with a protective stop order, which preserves the trading capital against major losses.

The problem is precisely that fakeouts are now the rule and real breakouts usually the exception. The successful breakout must therefore provide a very high gain to compensate for the many small losses the false breakouts bring along. Breakout trading can therefore be very frustrating when you expect a high hit rate.

In addition, not every fakeout is to be considered equal. A fakeout contrary to the major trend is a much more interesting opportunity as a fakeout in the direction of the trend. The reason is simple. If the main trend is upward, a false breakout downward from the range down may be an excellent opportunity for a long position. The example in Crude Oil (Figure 1) illustrates this fact very well.

Some traders think (and I share this opinion!) that fakeouts against the major trend can be considered as the best trading opportunities you can find in today's markets. If only for reasons of risk-reward ratio. It is definitely worthwhile to engage with this setup as a swing trader. I will in this respect show several examples in this book.

False breakouts in the direction of the major trends are usually short-term trades. The best target price, which a trader may expect in this case, is the other end of the range. Therefore, if the resistance has been overcome in the short term, and the trader identifies this move as a fakeout and therefore goes short, then his target is the support of the range.

In this case, however, the trader should always be aware that this false breakout could only be the first attempt and that at any time a breakout in the direction of the trend could succeed very well. Reaching the target price (the other end of the range) is by no means guaranteed. So, always keep the big picture in mind when you trade fakeouts.

Image 2: FDAX, 4-hour chart, Heikin Ashi

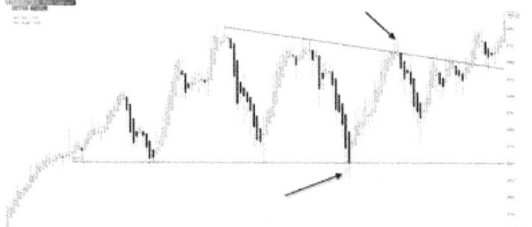

In this example, in the **FDAX** we first see a false breakout against the trend (arrow down). The aim of the trade was the upper end of the range, which has actually been achieved (reached?). The second false breakout took place in the direction of the major trend (arrow on the top). The target of the trade was the support line below. This target was not achieved, and we see that after two more attempts at real upside, breakout finally succeeded (in the direction of the major trend).

The trader therefore must continually remember that he can trade against the major trend though, the better chances are usually found with the trend.

How do I trade Fakeouts?

Any trading strategy should have clear rules and the "Trade the Fake strategy" is no exception. Identifying fakeouts belongs to the advanced strategies; the trader will have to deal with losing trades as anywhere else. It is therefore imperative that you apply the rules of risk and money management here also.

Above all, you should track trades with good risk-reward ratios. An RRR of 1: 2 is probably the minimum that you should achieve, better would be of course 1: 3 or even higher. I have summarized below some important points that I consider when trading the Trade the Fake strategy. They are not set in stone and there are certainly variations that I have not mentioned. Nevertheless, that will do to get you started in this strategy. With experience, you will itself be able to recognize fakeouts on charts and develop your own setups.

1. Look for consolidation zones in the chart. You can recognize these if the price moves in a narrow range, and so hold little volatility.

2. If possible, try to make the range visible using trend lines draw. At least two contacts with the line should occur, so that it is legitimized. The more touches the better.

3. Do not try to trade the breakout from this range, but wait on whether the breakout succeeds or whether it is a fakeout.

4. Having identified a fakeout; you open after the breakout candle a position in the opposite direction of

the breakout. If the closing price of the candle is still outside of the range, wait for the next candle (s), because in this case, it could be a successful breakout.

5. In the latter case, the market should relatively speedily return into the range. In the 4-hour chart, this should be done after 3-5 candles at the latest. If not, I would rather forego trading it.

6. Price target for short trades is the range support (bottom line of the range). Price target for long trades is the range resistance (upper line).

7. The stop, you should always put somewhat above the high of the fake candle (with upward breakouts) and somewhat under the fake candle (with downward breakouts).

8. You should at least reach a risk reward ratio of 1:2. 2 If the distance to the stop for example is 50 pips, your price target should be at least 100 pips away. If not, I would give up the trade.

It is important that you see no explosive eruption; the resistance breaks vertically upward (or downward at a support). Because then it could be that market sentiment has actually changed and the breakout succeeds, or even you experience the start of a strong trend.

Rather, you should observe a smaller movement, preferably with a shadow under or above the candle. A good sign are the doji or spinning tops just after the breakout candle. These indicate a hesitant behavior after the breakout. In other words, if no real momentum happens, this could be an indication that you are dealing with a fakeout.

Image 3: doji and spinning tops

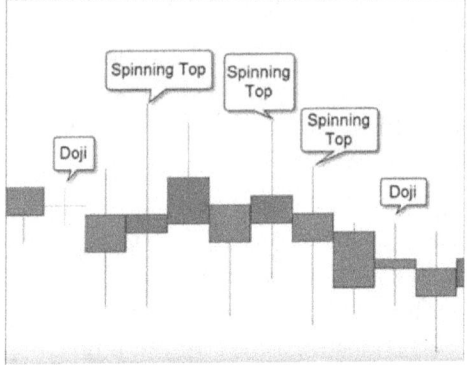

Especially when the news is thin, you should be skeptical about breakouts. What the catalyst could be, if not exactly important news changes, the perception of a market by the market participants thus enables a new trend. In the absence of such a catalyst, you should rather expect false breakouts.

In summary, the **following criteria** can be defined:

- A meaningful and verifiable support or resistance must be determined (minimum two touches)
- A false breakout or fakeout has caught on the wrong foot many market players.
- The support (or resistance) needs to be recaptured in the shortest possible time. The shorter the better.

These criteria are simple and clear. Nevertheless, I will illustrate this phenomenon in this book using several examples so that you are able to identify this when studying the charts yourself.

An important rule we can see in image 1 however: the faster the fakeout occurs (here within a 4-

hour candle) the more significant the subsequent move in the other direction could be.

The example in image 1 shows this impressively. The low of January 29th was US $ 43.57. If you went long $ 44.20 after the fakeout on the support and had put a stop loss order at US $ 43.50, you would be taking a risk of US $ 0.70. In the top you could have had a potential gain up to $ 10.

In other words, you are risking 70 cents for a potential profit of $ 10. You would therefore have entered a trade with a risk reward ratio of 1:14. These are exceptional opportunities, and I think that when swing trading you should try to identify precisely such extraordinary opportunities. Because that is what we are talking about, when we speak about trading.

Figure 4: EUR/JPY 4-hour chart

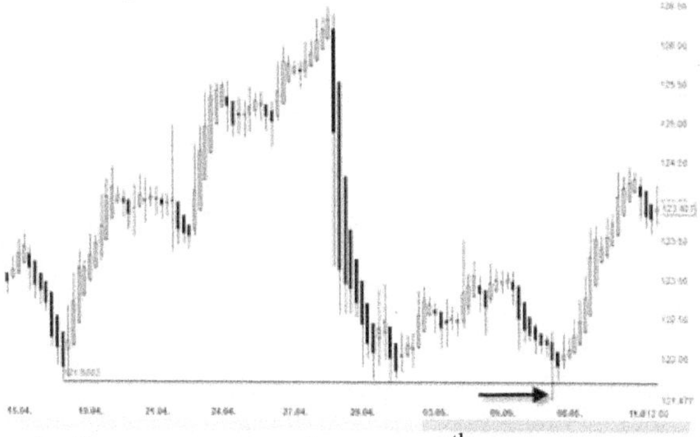

A similar case opened up on 6th of May 2016 in **EUR/JPY**. Here, "the market" broke for a short time the support at 121.70 and soared briefly to 121.47. These were admittedly only 23 pips, but again, we then see a significant rally over 200 pips in the opposite direction.

In this case, I would have bought after the breakout candle at about 122 and had a stop placed at 121.40, i.e. slightly below the low of the fakeout.

Therefore, I would have risked 60 pips. As you can see, USD/JPY went up over 124. Therefore, you are risking 60 pips to gain 200 and thus achieve a risk reward ratio of about 1: 3.

If to the classical doctrine you had bought the support with the second touch (middle of the chart), your profit would have been considerably more modest. It mostly pays to keep an eye out for a fakeout to get a real good chance.

Figure 5: E-mini, 4-hour chart Heikin Ashi

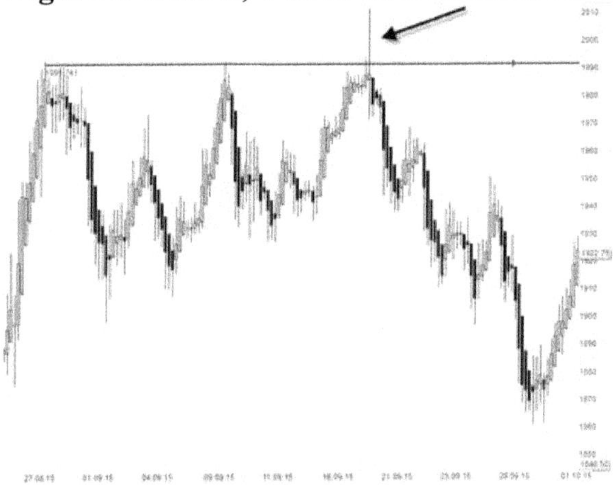

What is true for long positions, also applies to short positions of course, as this example in the **E-mini SP futures** clearly shows. In this case we see that the market encounter the psychologically important level of 2000 points as a clear resistance at 1992.75 (horizontal line above). This level was tested three times, until the "bulls" on September 17, 2015, started to attack the 2000 Level (arrow). You can clearly see how this price level was actually achieved for a short time and even exceeded. However, prices fell within a few hours back below the resistance.

This movement shows us a clear failure of the "bulls". We now know that it has probably dealt a feint on those traders who had previously placed large sell orders at the 2000 level. They just had to wait for "the market" to visit this level briefly so that their sell orders could be executed.

This fakeout in the E-Mini turned out to be an excellent short opportunity, which was good for at least 50 points. I would have secured the position with a stop at 2001 points, because, if the market would have reached this level a second time, the breakout may have succeeded.

Risking 10 points to gain 50 belongs to the good trading habits of swing traders. This corresponds to a risk reward ratio of 1: 5. You should try as a swing trader to achieve such RRRs. You will increase your profitability and merely need a hit rate of 50% in order to build a very profitable trading business.

Fakes with technical chart patterns

Now that we know the basic pattern of fakes, we can track them in different market situations. They generally occur on distinctive technical chart points, because the smart money knows that many retail investors look here for entry opportunities. In addition, of course, there are many stop-loss orders near those levels, and it is, as we have already seen, for the smart money an easy thing to take out these stops.

Do not let yourself be caught and learn to see through the game of the Smart Money. Every now and then, you can look at their cards and then you should snap at the chance. As a small fish, you can go swimming with those sharks, and I assure you, the spoils will be worth it!

A. flags

Figure 5: USD/JPY, 4-hour chart

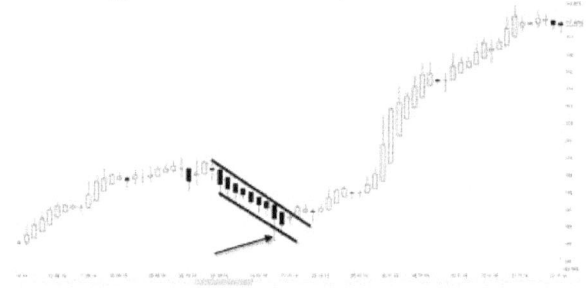

In this example, the USD/JPY (US Dollar - Japanese Yen) some market participants play their game with the expectations of classical technical analysis. The

USD/JPY was in a clear upward trend (white candles left in the chart), which was, as usual, separated by a short, clearly identifiable consolidation (black candles in the middle of the chart).

Those consolidation phases are usually opposing movements against the trend, which are usually resolved in the direction of the main trend. In this case, technical analysis speaks of a **"bullish flag"** because the previous upward trend looks like a flagpole and the opposing consolidation as the flag. Of course, there are also bearish flags.

Technical analysts like to draw the pattern with two trend lines because this brief consolidation often runs in a narrow trend channel as well as here in the USD/JPY. The classical expectation is now that this trend channel is resolved upwards. This would be done at a break of the upper channel line. This would be the buy signal for another wave of the upward movement.

However, as we can see, the opposite happened first. The lower channel line was broken down, triggering a sell signal. After all, this "break" was good for about 100 pips. This slip should therefore have caught many trend followers who had set their stop too closely to the market.

In addition, in this example, we see, however, that the "seller" soon leaves the field for new "buyers", who buffered the slip and bought the market back within the small trend channel. After a further consolidation candle within the channel a doji then appeared, and the next candle was then the expected breakout candle that triggered the buy signal according to the classical doctrine.

Whoever observed the fakeout and therefore the intention of those actors who had staged it, would have already bought once the courses were again within the channel. The fake trader knows that very strong hands now (Smart Money) would catch the USD/JPY at any time, as soon as he reached the bottom of the channel. The protective stop could have been placed just below the lower shadow of the fakeout.

In this way, the smart swing trader might come at a much cheaper price in the market than would have been the case if he had waited for the breakout. He had worked out a much better risk-reward ratio than the breakout trader who would have to place his stop below the channel. So here also, a close monitoring of the action would have led to a smarter trading decision.

Regarding the exits, I would clearly hold me in such a trend to the color of the Heikin Ashi charts. In this case, more than 1000 pips would have been a monster profit in this pair.

B. Triangles

Triangles are also among the classical instruments of the technical analysts. They generally belong to the so-called continuation patterns. This means that the expectation of the analysts is that a breakout of this geometric pattern will take place in the direction of the major trend.

Figure 6: DAX, 4-hour chart, Candlestick

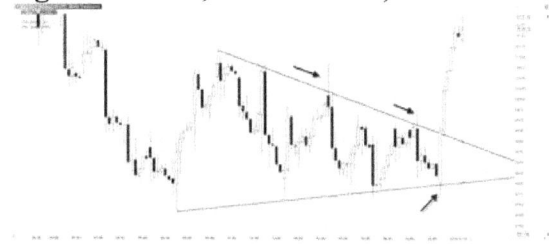

This image of the 4-hour chart of the DAX illustrates this. We see how the index runs into a symmetrical triangle after a falling trend. This is characterized by the decrease in volatility. Initially, the volatility is still large, but it is gradually reduced. The highs are lower and the lows higher, whereby the pattern was possible. The technical analyst, recognizing the pattern, distinguishes it in the chart mostly by two converging lines.

In this example, there were initially even more fakeouts. Twice, attempts were made to break through the resistance line upwards (arrows above). This failed twice. A swing trader could have gone short here twice. The target price was every time, the support line of the symmetrical triangle.

Now, it is the special feature of a symmetrical triangle that the trading range, as long as it exists, is always getting closer to. A decision thus forcing itself into one or the other direction.

The third attempt to break up then succeeded very well, and was indeed convincing. We see clearly how the bullish candles blow the resistance line unopposed. The trader should hence not oppose such a demonstration of the power of the bulls. Just the breakout candle itself encompassed the whole range. If you look at the reluctance of the market before the outbreak, you will understand that here something crucial changed. The candles are at once clearly without significant shadow. In addition, they are larger than most of the foregoing ones.

The expectation of the market participants was that the symmetrical triangle as a continuation pattern would be resolved downwards. This happened also in the fourth contact, but "the market" fell below the line only briefly. Short after that the massive upward movement started that triggered the actual breakout.

The downward fakeout as such meant the start of the upward breakout. This is also a classic faint you will see repeatedly in today's markets. It is almost normal that the first time the price seems to go in the wrong direction before the true intention is then apparent. Therefore, fake trading is such an exciting and rewarding business in my eyes.

C. Trend Channels

Figure 7: NZD/USD, 4-hour chart, Heikin Ashi

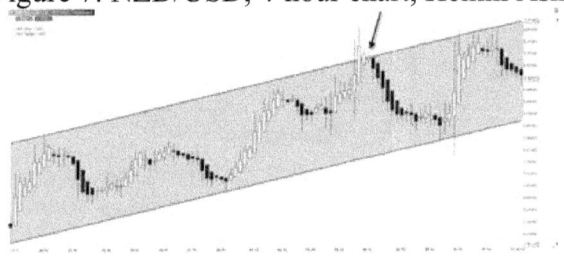

Trend channels are also the favorite tools of the technical analyst. They are sensible and practical tools, which are now integrated in almost all good platforms.

The principle is simple. Once the analyst has identified a trend, like those higher lows as in Figure 6 he can examine whether a parallel trend line can connect the highs of the trend.

In this case, in the currency pair **NZD/USD** (New Zealand Dollar - US dollar) this was indeed the case. Currencies incidentally like to move in such a trend channel. Every touch, be it with the bottom line or support line, or with the upper line or resistance line, provides an opportunity for the trader to make a profitable trade. Target price usually, is the next contact with the opposite line.

Traders who like to trade trend channels have their stops mostly either above the upper line (for short positions) or below the support line (for long positions). Since major players know this, they like to make a short "excursion" over or under one of the two lines to see how many stop orders they can fish this way.

Before they do so, they have long since placed larger orders that have exactly the opposite intention. If they shoot over the top, as in this example, they drive prices so far upwards until their short orders are executed through the resistance line. Under pressure of the sell orders, the price comes back and end up back inside the channel. A Smart scalper may smell a rat and jump on the falling train, which further accelerates the trend.

The advanced way to trade trend channels would not in the classical sense, be to trade the next touch, but to wait and see whether or not some fakeout emerges, which represents a much stronger elastic spring in the other direction, as it may be the classic touch. If breakout traders fell for the fakeout they will think twice whether to go long again after the smart money has taken them out of the market.

Therefore, it might be wise to rather wait until the stops were fished and breakout traders have been caught on the wrong foot, to enter into a position within the trend channel. The trader has thus a much stronger confirmation of the rejection. In addition, he is trading in the same direction as the Smart Money that would now drive the market toward the other channel line again.

What is interesting in the above example in figure 7, after the breakout "failed" the heikin ashi chart draws a doji (arrow above), whose closing price was exactly under the support line. Thus, the "buyers" failed to hold the market outside the channel. In this case, after completion of the doji- 4-hour candle a short position would have been the logical conclusion.

Therefore, if the trader went short at the opening price of the next candle (at 0.6733), they could put a stop-loss order somewhere at the high of the fakeout (at 0.6790). He would therefore have a risk of 57 pips. Target price was then the lower edge of the channel, which at that time was a level roughly around the round number of 0.6600. The trader risked 57 pips to win the 133. This corresponds to a risk-reward ratio of 1: 2.33. This RRR is indeed significantly lower than in the previous examples, fakeouts in trend channels are but excellent trading opportunities that have a high degree probability of winning.

Trading cross rates

Figure 8: CAD/JPY daily chart, Heikin Ashi

It may well make sense from time to time to see beyond one's own nose and trade markets that are not in the focus of the international traders community. You usually hear nothing or almost nothing in the press and on the internet of enough interesting markets. As they find less observation, the trader will usually experience less "competition".

Often, this means that the trends are better and the rules of technical analysis function better. However, don't let yourself be fooled: here too, or perhaps rather here, big players are on the road, as the above example of the CAD/JPY (Canadian Dollar - Japanese Yen) clearly shows.

If I trade the so-called cross rates (currency pairs, where the US dollar is not one of the currencies), I like to watch as a swing trader on the daily chart. This often gives me a long-term perspective over several years. I can see how the big players trade those currencies. Here you will often find daunting trends that can last years.

So it pays well, to deal with these markets. I prefer to watch those charts on weekends, usually on

Sundays. Then, I am not involved in daily operations and two days of abstinence from the stock market gives me the necessary distance to see things that I overlooked during the week.

If we consider this example in CAD/JPY in more detail, we see here again a classic false downside breakout after the pair had found a support at 71 (bottom horizontal line). The break of this support lasted only two days.

The long shadows under the two black Heikin Ashi candles suggest that buyers caught this market again (we know these buyers now). The further development of the chart clearly shows that this fakeout was exactly the start of the upward trend that followed. What you see (downward breakout, arrow), is the exact opposite of what was actually intended.

After the smart money had covered with CAD/JPY lots at the low, they started to trade this pair up, day after day. Then, there were even another two good opportunities for fake traders to get in the market at a good price (two arrows on the right). Again, the big players helped diligently to keep the price within the trend channel.

More complex patterns

Figure 9: EUR/JPY daily chart

Figure 9 shows the heikin ashi view of the daily chart of the EUR/JPY. This section covers the period of December 2013 to August 2015. Experienced technical analysts recognize it relatively quickly on a chart: this is the inner or internal trend line that often shows a reversal of roles between support and resistance. From December 2013 to November 2014, the line clearly served as a resistance. The bulls never succeeded to overcome this line. Once they succeeded on 19/09/2014. Nevertheless, this breakout proved itself as a fakeout (first left arrow).

Between November 2014 and January 2015, the pair then managed a significant breakout above the resistance line. Nevertheless, it returned to the line and fell back under it. Surprisingly, the line after this excursion was still valid and acted several times as further resistance. After two more fakeouts (arrows 2 and 3), the pair fell back until it finally on May 3rd, 2015 overcame the resistance line again, this time successfully.

After this date, the function of the line turned around. From now on, it functioned as a support. In addition, here we see two fakes, which could be traded very well.

Figure 10: EUR/JPY daily chart heikin ashi, April 2015 - June 2016

Figure 10 shows the second part of this chart. The incredible thing is that the internal trend line since December 2013 still had its validity. The EUR/JPY still oscillates around it. Sometimes, it acts as a support, sometimes as resistance. Up until the date of this screenshot (June 2. 2016), the line still remained valid. Thus, it is expected to continue its contacts and fakes.

Of course, trend lines or internal trend lines with duration of over two years are rare, but they exist. This internal trend line here shows the shallow downtrend in EUR/JPY since two and a half years.

With practice, the trader will be able to recognize similar internal trend lines on other charts. They are so interesting, because market players seem to respect them over long periods. Sometimes, the touches are precise, but often the Smart Money likes to stage a fakeout. These are then usually excellent trading opportunities.

Glossary

Bullish Flag: Short-term movement in opposite direction against the main trend.
Candlesticks: Coding of price changes on the basis of a Japanese analysis technology.
Continuation pattern: Break in the main trend at the conclusion of which previous direction is resumed.
Cross rates: Currency pairs, where the US dollar is not one of the two currencies.
Doji: Candlestick formation by which the opening and closing prices are at the same level.
E-Mini Futures: Futures contract on the American index SP500.
Forex: Forex Exchange Market, international foreign exchange market.
Hammer: Reversal candle in the candlestick representation. The candle has a small body with a long shadow down.
Heikin Ashi chart: "Balancing on one foot" Japanese representation form of price changes.
Internal trend line: A trend line, which function changes from resistance to support.
Interest rate decision: Announcement of central bank's decisions about the future course of interest rates.
Long Position: To be Long's means to have purchased securities and thus own them.
Momentum: The momentum informs the investor about the pace and strength of a price movement.
Money Management: Money Management refers to a strategy, which aims to control the risk of the securities

portfolio by size determination of the individual trading positions.

Pip: Percentage in point, the smallest change in the price in currency trading.

Range: A clear defined trading range over a given period.

Risk Management: Includes all measures for the systematic identification, analysis, evaluation, monitoring and controlling of risks.

Risk-reward ratio (RRR): The RRR is an indicator of the usefulness of a system. It is calculated by dividing the expected profitability of the maximum loss.

Scalping: Trading technique by which the trader trades minimal movements in the market.

Short position: A trader is short when he sells a position without owning them (short sale).

Sell-Stop order: Automatic sell order that is triggered when the market reaches that price level.

Spinning Top: Chart pattern with a small body and long shadows.

Stop Fishing: Late apparent movement of larger market players to trigger the stops of small investors.

Stop Loss Order: Sell order, which is carried out once a certain price is reached.

Trend Following: Trading strategy, which focuses on the following of a once identified trend.

Support: Price level at which buyers increasingly emerge.

Volatility: Standard deviation. Specifies how the price of a market varies.

Resistance: Price level at which increased sellers emerge.

Other Books by Heikin Ashi Trader

Swing Trading with the 4-hour chart
Part 3: Where do I put my stop?

In the third, part of the series on "Swing Trading with the 4-hour chart" the Heikin Ashi Trader answers to the question of where the stop should be placed. Once a trader introduces stops in his system, his hit rate will deteriorate. However, at the same time he gains full control of the trade management. Stops are therefore not unavoidable but an integral part of a trading system that is profit-oriented.

Well understood stops are downright the actual instrument that makes a profit possible. Since money is only earned when he exits the trade, the trader would do well to conduct the stop management with the utmost care. The formulation of crystal-clear rules, both with trading the trend as in trading with a fixed target price, after all, is the requirement to ensure that the trader is playing his own game.

Every successful trader has eventually developed its own rules. No matter what the market, this trader always plays his own game and cannot be swayed by anything. Exactly the persistence and consistency with which these traders operate in the market ensures that they become one day the "Master of the Game".

Table of Contents

1. Are stops necessary?
2. What is a Stop Loss Order?
3. Stop management
4. Play your own game
5. Limiting losses
6. Letting profits run
7. Stop management in trending markets
8. Stop management with price targets
9. The Swiss franc tsunami, a healing moment for the trader community
10. How many positions I can keep at the same time?

About the Author

Heikin Ashi Trader is recognized worldwide as the specialist in scalping with the Heikin Ashi chart. He has been trading this way for 19 years. He traded for a hedge fund and then went into business for himself as a trader. His scalping book "Scalping is Fun!" is an international bestseller and has been sold more than 30,000 times. You can find more information about his scalping method on his website www.heikinashitrader.net

Imprint

Texts: © Copyright by Heikin Ashi Trader
Swiss Post Box 106287
Zürcher Strasse 161
CH-8010 Zürich
Switzerland
All rights reserved.

www.ingramcontent.com/pod-product-compliance
Lightning Source LLC
Chambersburg PA
CBHW070228210526
45169CB00023B/1359